# What Was Pompeii?

# What Was Pompeii?

by Jim O'Connor

illustrated by John Hinderliter

Grosset & Dunlap
An Imprint of Penguin Group (USA) LLC

To Pliny, who first told about the
eruption of Mount Vesuvius—JOC

To Dee Dee, thank you for the
love and support—JH

GROSSET & DUNLAP
Published by the Penguin Group
Penguin Group (USA) LLC, 375 Hudson Street, New York, New York 10014, USA

USA | Canada | UK | Ireland | Australia | New Zealand | India | South Africa | China

penguin.com
A Penguin Random House Company

Text copyright © 2014 by Jim O'Connor. Illustrations copyright © 2014 by John
Hinderliter. Cover illustration copyright © 2014 by Fred Harper. All rights reserved.
Published by Grosset & Dunlap, a division of Penguin Young Readers Group,
345 Hudson Street, New York, New York 10014. GROSSET & DUNLAP
is a trademark of Penguin Group (USA) LLC. Printed in the USA.

*Library of Congress Cataloging-in-Publication Data is available.*

ISBN 978-0-448-47907-1                    10 9 8 7 6 5 4 3 2 1

# Contents

# What Was Pompeii?

On the morning of August 24, 79 AD, the people in the town of Pompeii went about their normal routines. It seemed like any other day. Shopkeepers opened up their stores. In the center of town, people gathered in the Forum to discuss politics and shop at the outdoor market. Others prayed in one of the many temples to the Roman gods and goddesses.

In other parts of the city, people went to the public baths and played sports. Just outside Pompeii, farmers tended their fields. They grew olives and grapes and tended flocks of sheep. The land around Pompeii was rich and fertile.

A little farther away, five miles from town, stood Vesuvius. Vesuvius looked like a mountain. But it wasn't a mountain. It was a volcano. No one in Pompeii worried about Vesuvius. It hadn't erupted in seven hundred years. However, in the past weeks there had been small earthquakes. People could feel the ground shaking under their feet.

Still, no one in Pompeii expected anything terrible to happen. No one guessed that the earthquakes were a warning sign. Vesuvius was about to erupt. And when it did erupt, early in the afternoon of August 24, it destroyed the entire

town of Pompeii. By the end of the following day, Pompeii had disappeared under sixty feet of volcanic ash. It was as if the town had never existed.

# The Roman Empire

Pompeii was a thriving harbor city located at the mouth of the Sarno River on the Bay of Naples, and it was part of the Roman Empire. By the end of the first century AD, the vast Roman Empire stretched from Great Britain through France, Germany, Italy, Greece, east across the Mediterranean Sea into what are now the countries of Iraq, Israel, and Egypt, and down into North Africa. Rome was the center of the empire and the most important city. (Pompeii was 150 miles south of Rome.) A network of paved roads connected many outlying areas to Rome. Roman boats crisscrossed the Mediterranean Sea carrying spices, cloth, wine, olive oil, and other goods to all parts of the empire. The powerful Roman army and navy kept order for the emperor, who ruled with absolute power.

Atlantic Ocean

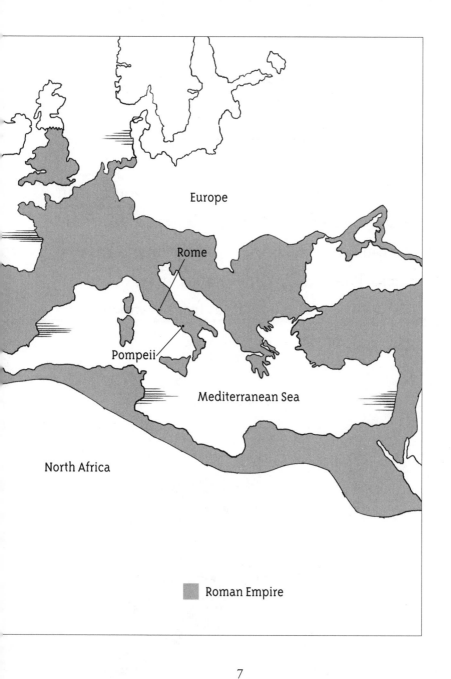

Europe

Rome

Pompeii

Mediterranean Sea

North Africa

Roman Empire

# CHAPTER 1
## Eyewitness

On that terrible day in 79 AD, a young man watched Vesuvius erupting. He was called Pliny the Younger. (His uncle was known as Pliny the Elder.) Pliny was a safe distance away, in a town just across the Bay of Naples from Pompeii.

In a couple letters written many years later, he described everything that he saw. What Pliny wrote is the only eyewitness account of the destruction of Pompeii.

". . . in the early afternoon my mother drew attention to a cloud of unusual size and appearance. . . . It was not clear at that distance from which mountain the cloud was rising. (It was afterwards known to be Vesuvius.) Its general appearance can best be expressed as being like an umbrella pine, for it rose to a great height on a sort of trunk and then split off into branches. . . . It spread out and gradually dispersed. In places it looked white, elsewhere blotched and dirty."

Pliny's description is an accurate one. However, he could only see what was happening from afar. He had no way of knowing what effect the eruption had on all the people living in Pompeii. To them, it must have seemed as if they were witnessing the end of the world. When Vesuvius erupted, it shot up a column of dark ash and sharp, lightweight powdery rock called *pumice*. (You say it like this: puhm-iss.) The column rose about 15,000 feet into the air. (That's about three miles high.) The winds blew the ash and rocks toward Pompeii, turning the sky pitch-black.

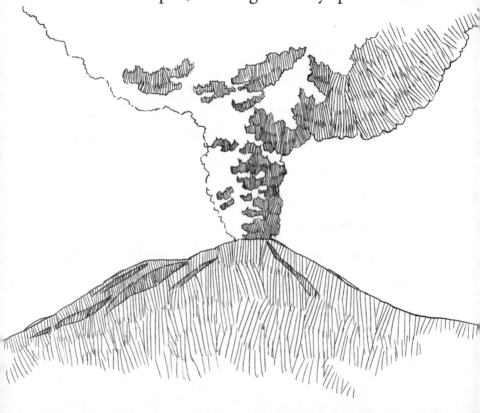

Anyone caught at home had no chance of surviving. They were buried by the falling ash and rocks. Many of those who managed to get past the city gates didn't survive, either. They, too, were caught in the hot downpour and suffocated. Before the eruption, there had been almost 20,000 people living in Pompeii. About 2,000 were killed inside the city. But there is simply no way to know how many others died trying to escape. For

eighteen hours the ash and rock kept falling, layer
upon layer. It piled up until sixty feet covered the
city. Sixty feet! That's the height of a five-story
building! Soon there was no trace of Pompeii.

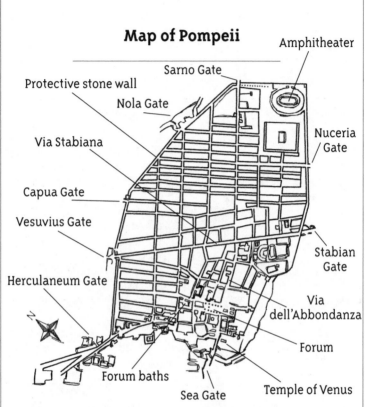

# Map of Pompeii

Amphitheater

Protective stone wall

Sarno Gate

Nola Gate

Via Stabiana

Nuceria Gate

Capua Gate

Vesuvius Gate

Herculaneum Gate

Stabian Gate

Via dell'Abbondanza

Forum

Forum baths

Sea Gate

Temple of Venus

This map shows where the important streets, famous houses, public buildings, and major temples were located. Pompeii was circled by a stone wall. This was to protect the town from enemies. People entered and departed from Pompeii through one of the gates in the wall.

# CHAPTER 2
## What Is a Volcano?

From far away, a volcano looks a lot like an ordinary mountain. When a volcano is erupting, however, red-hot liquid rock called lava spews from the top; ash and poison gases are released. The lava flows downward, destroying everything in its path. At Vesuvius, in 79 AD, the lava hardened in the air into sharp rocks that rained down on the people of Pompeii.

If you climbed up Vesuvius, right away you would see that, as with many volcanoes, there is a big hole at the top. What made the hole?

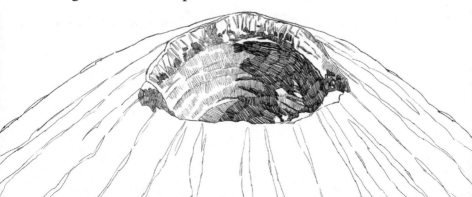

The crust is the name for the earth's top layer and is made up of many huge pieces called plates.

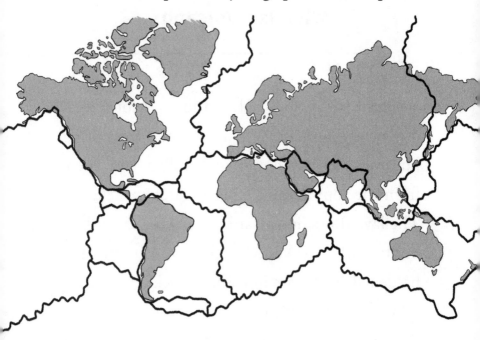

The plates move and float on top of very hot melted rock. When this melted rock finds a crack between plates, it bubbles up, up, up through a tube and bursts out of the ground, punching out a hole. This kind of hole is called a crater. Once the liquid rock spurts out of the crater, it is called lava. The lava cools and hardens, creating a hill around the crater. With each eruption of lava at Vesuvius, the hill of the volcano grew bigger and taller.

There are three kinds of volcanoes. Active volcanoes erupt regularly. Kilauea in Hawaii has been erupting for the last thirty years. Mauna Loa, also in Hawaii, is the largest volcano, taller even than Mount Everest. There are about 1,500 potentially active volcanoes on the earth. (Some are underwater in oceans.) Dormant volcanoes are ones that have not erupted in the last 10,000 years. (*Dormant* means sleeping.) However, scientists can still detect some activity inside them, which means they might erupt again at some point. Yellowstone in Wyoming is a dormant volcano. Extinct volcanoes are no longer active, and scientists think it is very unlikely that they will ever erupt again. Edinburgh Castle in Scotland sits on top of an extinct volcano. The eruption of Vesuvius was very destructive, killing at least 2,000 people, but other eruptions have been much more deadly. In 1883, Krakatoa in Indonesia erupted, killing 40,000 people. The last time that Vesuvius erupted was in 1944. Pompeii was unharmed. Today vineyards flourish in the rich volcanic soil on the slopes of Vesuvius.

# The World's Most Active Volcanoes

Spirit Lake

Etna in Sicily has been continuously erupting for 3,500 years. It is the largest volcano in Europe.

Stromboli, a volcano on an island off the coast of Italy, has been continuously erupting for 2,000 years. That makes it the second most active volcano. Stromboli started as an undersea volcano, and after many eruptions it became an island.

Forest obliterated

Mount Yasur on Vanuatu Island in the South Pacific ranks as the third most active volcano. It has been continuously erupting for eight hundred years.

The next most active are Santa Maria in Guatemala, Central America; and Piton de la Fouaise which is on Réunion Island in the west Indian Ocean.

Mount St. Helens in the state of Washington is

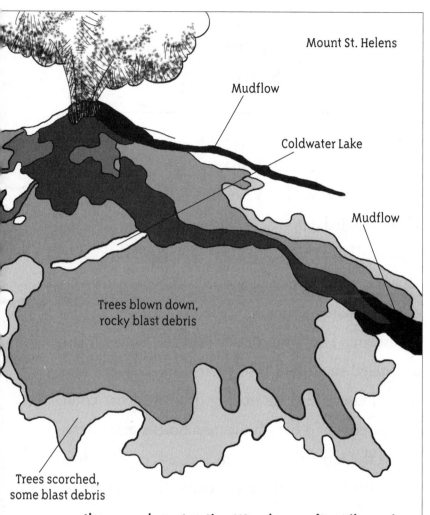

Mount St. Helens

Mudflow

Coldwater Lake

Mudflow

Trees blown down,
rocky blast debris

Trees scorched,
some blast debris

the second most active US volcano after Kilauea in Hawaii. Its 1980 eruption buried two hundred square miles of forest and killed 57 people.

# CHAPTER 3
## A Buried City

Some people did manage to escape from the destruction of Vesuvius. If they returned to Pompeii later on, it was not to rebuild their houses. There was no hope of that. Pompeii as they had known it was gone forever. Survivors came to search for valuables left behind in the rush to escape. They dug down into the volcanic ash and tried to tunnel into their homes. They took away material like marble and bronze that could be reused when they built new homes elsewhere.

At the same time, looters arrived, eager to steal whatever things of value could be unearthed. They, too, dug tunnels to houses. Tunneling, however, was very dangerous. Sometimes the tunnels collapsed and killed whoever was inside

them. After a while, the area where Pompeii lay buried was left abandoned. All the survivors and all the children of the survivors died off. Looters stopped coming. And eventually there was no one alive who remembered the town or what it had been like to live there. Pompeii was no longer seen as a real place. It became a myth—a city that had vanished. Over time the layers of volcanic ash turned into soil—fertile soil that was good for growing crops. So the land above the lost city became covered with farms and vineyards once again. People began to call the area *Civitas* which means *city*. They were living and farming on top of ancient ruins, though no one knew that.

# Pliny and His Letters

Pliny the Younger became a lawyer, a government official, and an author. He lived in Italy and died in 113 AD in Turkey. He loved writing letters; he wrote hundreds, including the ones about the destruction of Pompeii. Almost all of Pliny's letters discussed his work as an administrator, judge, and diplomat. The two letters about Pompeii were ignored or passed over for more than 1,500 years. Around 1600, the letters were finally found. Until then there was no way for anyone to know what had happened that awful August day in 79 AD.

## CHAPTER 4
## Discoveries

In 1599, workers digging a tunnel under Civitas came upon something very surprising—walls with pictures painted on them and some marble slabs. The worker in charge of the tunnel-digging thought perhaps they had come upon ruins from an ancient Roman house. But no one bothered to investigate any further.

More than a hundred years later, in 1748, an engineer named Rocque Joaquín de Alcubierre arrived at the same spot with a crew of twenty-four men. The king of Naples was building a museum. The king hoped to fill it with treasures from ancient Roman times.

Not very far from Civitas, Alcubierre and his team had unearthed some treasures. But everything had been encased in rock that was

as hard as cement. It was terribly difficult to dig anything out. So Alcubierre decided to try excavating in Civitas instead, where the layers of ash and pumice were much easier to dig through. Although Alcubierre was disappointed by the few things discovered, he left a small team to continue digging. In 1750, a young engineer joined the men at Civitas. His name was Karl Weber.

Alcubierre had used crude methods to try to unearth objects—often he used explosives. He also kept no records of what he discovered or where it had been found. Weber was different. He understood that history might be lying preserved right under his feet. Digging had to be done carefully, layer by layer, starting at the top and working slowly downward. Also, he kept a log of where and when every object was found. Weber's methods are still used by archaeologists today. (An archaeologist studies objects from the past in order to learn about the people and culture of a particular time.)

Karl Weber began supervising the digging at Civitas. It took five years before he made a major discovery. His men unearthed a large town house. They named it the House of Julia Felix. The house covered an area of an entire city block!

In 1763, Weber made two more significant discoveries in Pompeii: the Herculaneum Gate and the Via delle Tombe, or Street of Tombs. During this time Weber also mapped out an important house, the Villa of the Papyri in a nearby Roman town.

Until then, the king of Naples hadn't been much interested in the excavation at Civitas. But now he was! He directed Weber to continue the work there, and his careful work paid off. Slowly tunneling down through volcanic ash, the workers uncovered the remains of a crowded ancient Roman town. There had been two main streets that crossed each other. Archeologists named them the Via dell'Abbondanza (that's Italian for Street of Plenty) and Via Stabiana, which led in the direction of the nearby town of Stabia.

On Via dell'Abbondanza were the ruins of many homes, shops, and restaurants. Many side streets, also filled with homes and stores, branched off from the Via dell'Abbondanza in a neat grid. Clearly this had once been a prosperous town.

For years the digging went on. Then, in 1763, an inscription reading "Rei publicae

REI·PUBLICAE·POMPEIANORUM

Pompeianorum" was found. In Latin, the language of the Romans, these words meant "the Commonwealth of Pompeii." Here was clear proof that identified the site as Pompeii. Weber and his men were not uncovering just any town from ancient Roman times. They had found Pompeii, the city that Vesuvius had destroyed!

# CHAPTER 5
## More Discoveries

Karl Weber died suddenly in 1764 and was replaced by Francesco La Vega. Under his direction, more and more of Pompeii was revealed. La Vega's discovery of a Roman temple in 1764 made him famous. It was the most complete Roman temple ever found. It had not been looted and had all its furnishings and some spectacular frescoes, which are paintings done right on walls.

In Pompeii the largest places of worship were the Temple of Apollo, the Temple of Venus, and the Temple of Jupiter. The people of Pompeii believed that Venus was their special protector. Did they think that Venus had forsaken them on the day Vesuvius erupted?

Temple of Isis

## Gods and Goddesses

In Pompeii there were many temples where crowds could come and pray to the different Roman gods and goddesses. At home, people also kept small shrines so they could worship in private. The most powerful Roman gods were like superheroes. If ordinary humans did anything to displease them, the gods were quick to punish them.

Juno          Vulcan          Jupiter

Jupiter was the king of the gods. His wife was
Juno. They had many children who were also gods.
Mars was known as the god of war, Neptune was
the god of the sea, Venus was the goddess of love,
Apollo was the god of the sun, and Minerva was the
goddess of the moon. Vulcan was the god of fire.
From Vulcan comes the word *volcano*.

In 1860 Giuseppe Fiorelli was appointed Director of Excavations at Pompeii.

He already had been working at the site for twenty years. More than any other person, Fiorelli revealed the Pompeii that visitors see today. The first thing Fiorelli did as director was remove all the mounds of dirt and debris that previous digging teams had left in the streets of Pompeii.

Once this was done, the layout of Pompeii became clear. Visitors could more easily get a sense of the city as it had been before Vesuvius erupted. He also mapped out the city of Pompeii and came up with a system that identified the exact location of every house and shop.

By then about two-thirds of Pompeii, 15,000 buildings spread out over 110 acres, had been uncovered. Fiorelli strongly believed that all objects found should remain "in situ." (You say it

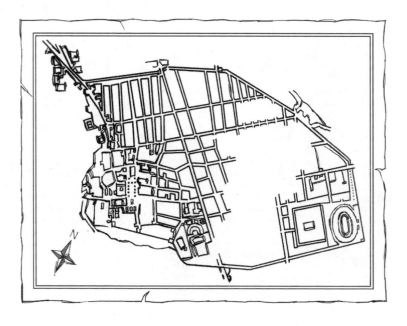

like this: in sigh-tyou.) That meant leaving them where they were found. He did not allow frescoes, statues, mosaics or anything else of value to be carted away or sold. He opened the site to anyone who could pay a small entrance fee. Before this, only rich and powerful people had been allowed into Pompeii.

The entrance fees paid for guards who watched over the site and prevented thieves from stealing

anything. Fiorelli also was responsible for what are the most disturbing and yet also the most fascinating exhibits at Pompeii—he made the first plaster casts of victims caught at the exact moment they died. Victims quickly were buried under the layers of ash raining down from Vesuvius. The ash hardened around their bodies. The bodies decayed over time until only a heap of bones remained for each victim. However, the hardened ash kept the original, hollowed-out shape of the body.

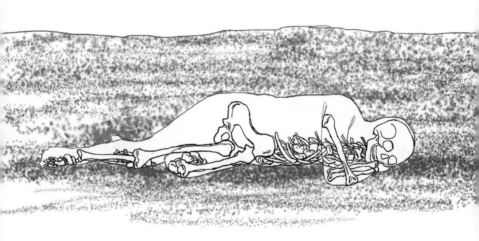

As soon as Fiorelli's workers, digging carefully, spotted anything that looked like it might be the outline of a body, they stopped digging. A hole was drilled into the hollow cavity. Then they poured in plaster of Paris and waited for it to harden. What the plaster produced were incredibly detailed and realistic replicas of victims of the volcano. Whole families were found trying vainly to escape. One man was trying to throw his cloak over his wife to protect her. Their children and servants lay near the couple. Looking at the casts, it is easy to make out even small details such as hairstyles or the type

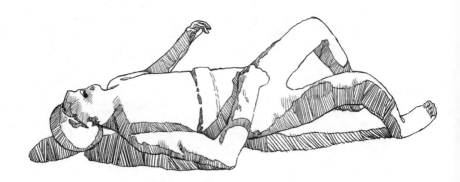

of sandals the person was wearing. One of the most famous casts is of a dog that was chained to a stake. He could not escape, and so he is caught, contorted, trying frantically to bite through the chain holding him.

## CHAPTER 6
## Shopping in Pompeii

Pompeii had a thriving business community. People worked at many different trades. There were metalsmiths, gem-cutters, sandal-makers, boot-makers, barbers, dentists, weavers, and bakers. In fact, there were about thirty bakeries

operating in town. Most of them had their own mills to grind flour. They used brick ovens that are somewhat similar to 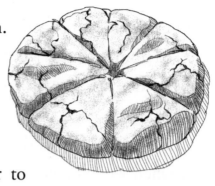 pizza ovens. The bigger bakeries had enormous ovens. One oven was unearthed—it had 81 loaves of bread still inside! The loaves were rounded and indented into eight sections for easy cutting.

Why was there a need for so many bakeries? It was because only the rich had kitchens in their homes. Poor people took their dough to a bakery and then returned later in the day, after it had been baked into bread, to take it home. Pompeians enjoyed drinking wine made from the grapes grown in the vineyards outside of town.

There were many taverns in town, as well as small restaurants and inns for travelers. The taverns usually were tiny—just a couple small rooms opening out onto the street. Food was served from large clay jars fitted into a countertop. Inside one tavern, dishes and food jars were unearthed as well as a kettle still containing a mixture of wine and water that was heating up when the volcano erupted. (Most people in Pompeii liked to drink their wine warm.) People seasoned meat, vegetables, and fruit with a

popular fish sauce called *garum*. (They also used *garum* for medicine.)

*Garum* was made from fermented fish intestines and had a strong, foul odor. It sounds awful, but making *garum* was very profitable. At the time of the eruption, a man named Scaurus produced the highest quality *garum* in all of Pompeii. Scaurus grew rich making *garum*. He lived in a large and luxurious house outside the city walls. When the house was uncovered, four large black-and-white mosaics were found in the entrance hall. (Mosaics are pictures made from small pieces of colored glass or clay.)

The mosaics depicted jars of Scaurus's famous *garum*. Scaurus obviously was proud of his product, which was exported throughout the empire. Some jars with labels reading "Scaurus's Finest Mackerel Sauce" were found as far away as France. Scaurus also produced kosher *garum* for Jewish customers.

The discovery of kosher *garum* suggests that Jews were living in Pompeii in the first century AD. No Jewish temple has been discovered, so their numbers were probably small. At the time of the eruption, Christianity also was spreading to parts of the Roman Empire. However, so far there is no evidence that Christians lived in Pompeii. Another big business in Pompeii was known as *fulling*. These shops took the raw cloth and cleaned, dyed, and softened it until it was ready to be made into togas and tunics. Fullers' shops also functioned as laundries for the townspeople.

# Pompeii Fashion

We think of the men of ancient Rome as all dressing in togas. But actually, not everyone was allowed to wear them. A toga could only be worn by a male citizen. Most togas were plain white, but important men in the government sported stripes on their togas. Slaves and former slaves called freedmen wore short wool tunics. Tunics were more comfortable and easier to move around in, which came in handy if you were a hardworking tradesman or soldier.

Women wore long tunics called *stolas*, sometimes both an inner and an outer one. They were usually made of wool or linen, although very rich women might have had clothing made of silk that came from China. As for children, they wore the same kind of clothing as their parents, only in smaller sizes, of course. In cold or rainy weather, Pompeians wore heavy wool cloaks. Many of the victims preserved in plaster in Pompeii are wearing cloaks, probably to protect themselves from the falling ash and pumice.

Wealthy Pompeians loved to wear jewelry, so metalsmiths could earn a good living if they were talented jewelers. The men of Pompeii kept it simple; they would wear one or possibly two rings. Women, however, liked to wear lots of jewelry— bracelets, rings, earrings, necklaces, and pins to fasten cloaks. Some bracelets and armbands were designed to look like snakes twisting around and around. The most expensive jewelry was made of gold and often decorated with colorful gemstones.

Young boys were given a locket called a *bulla* when they were nine days old. The *bulla* signified that they were born free men. A boy wore his *bulla* until he became a Roman citizen at the age of sixteen. Girls wore lockets called *lunulas* until the night before they got married. For someone with money, there were certainly wonderful goods to buy in Pompeii. Soft woolens, beautiful jewelry, finely made sandals, and sweet-smelling lotions for the skin. As you would expect, daily life was very different if you were poor and had to scrape by, earning only enough money to survive.

# CHAPTER 7
# Rich and Poor, Side by Side

In Pompeii, most buildings were no more than two stories high, and homes and shops were built side by side on city blocks. Even though most of them lost their roof or second floor in the eruption, there is no place where houses from ancient Roman times are better preserved.

Like every other city in the Roman Empire, Pompeii had a bad crime problem. There were no streetlights, so it was dangerous to be out walking at night. And although there were courts in the Forum, there doesn't seem to have been any type of police force. As a result of the high crime rate, most houses only had small windows set up high. This was to discourage intruders. Any larger windows facing the streets had grills of bronze or wood over them. At sundown homeowners locked their front doors, and shopkeepers locked up their shops.

In Pompeii, rich and poor lived side by side on the same block and often in the same building. But while the poor had to make do with one small, stuffy room for an entire family, rich Pompeians

built large and lavish homes where they enjoyed a
very pleasant life.

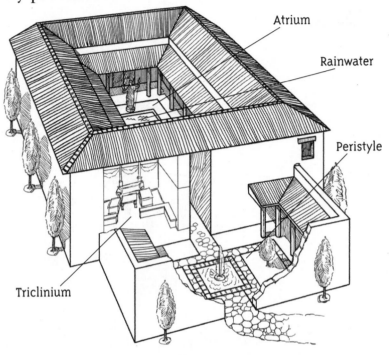

The ideal Roman house had a very specific
layout. An entrance hall led into an open-air
room called an *atrium*. It was common practice
for wealthy Romans to use their homes as a
place to conduct business. Customers and clients
waited in the atrium until the owner was ready

to see them. In the middle of the atrium was a shallow pool for collecting rain water that came in through a hole in the roof. The water was saved and used for cooking and washing. Behind the atrium was a large room with a roof where the owner of the house met visitors and discussed business. Bedrooms were often located off the atrium. They were small and usually did not have windows. The bathroom was very often a room with no more than a hole in the floor. Only the very biggest homes had their own baths.

Farther into the house was an enclosed garden or *peristyle*. Many peristyles had fountains and outdoor dining rooms. In larger houses there was also an indoor dining room called a *triclinium*. The well-to-do enjoyed fancy dinners at home with many kinds of food and lots of wine. A favorite dish was dormouse cooked in honey and sprinkled with poppy seeds!

In their elaborately decorated dining rooms, the hosts and their guests reclined on built-in benches or sofas while they ate. Each bench could hold three people. Pompeians did not use forks; they ate with their fingers. So during the course of a dinner party, which usually lasted many hours, people washed their hands many times.

Wealthy Pompeians decorated the walls of rooms with lavish frescoes. Most were painted in bright colors—blues, greens, and an intense red that is still called "Pompeian Red."

Fresco is a technique of mural-painting done on fresh, wet lime plaster. Once the paints and plaster dry, the painting becomes cemented into the wall. The word *fresco* means "fresh" in Italian, because the painter must work quickly before the fresh plaster dries. Frescoes often illustrated scenes of gods and goddesses. Some frescos were painted to create the illusion of a window opening onto a beautiful view of the countryside. And sometimes a fresco might be painted on the back wall of a garden to make it appear as if the garden was larger than it really was.

Homes of the rich also featured mosaics— pictures made of pieces of colored stone or glass, known as *tesserae*. (You say it like this: tess-uh-rye.) The pieces are set into plaster to form a design or scene. In Pompeii, intricate and beautiful mosaics were found on both the floors and walls of temples as well as houses.

The most famous mosaic found in Pompeii is the Alexander Mosaic that originally was on the floor of the House of the Faun. (Today it is displayed in a museum in Naples, and a copy is at Pompeii.) Measuring nineteen feet by ten feet three inches, it shows the Greek hero and king Alexander the Great defeating Darius, King of Persia, who is shown driving a chariot. More than one and a half million pieces were needed to complete the design!

Most mosaics in Pompeii were far smaller and often much simpler in their designs. In many houses, there would be a mosaic just inside the front door showing a fierce dog with the words "Cave Canem" (Beware of the Dog) underneath. It was one method of warning off robbers—whether there was actually a guard dog in the house or not!

Pompeian houses did not have a lot of furniture—just beds, a couple of wooden chairs, and cupboards, tables, and couches.

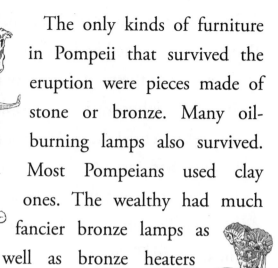

The only kinds of furniture in Pompeii that survived the eruption were pieces made of stone or bronze. Many oil-burning lamps also survived. Most Pompeians used clay ones. The wealthy had much fancier bronze lamps as well as bronze heaters called *braziers*. Wealthy Pompeians did not cook meals, clean their houses, or weed their gardens. All of that was done by slaves.

Slavery was common in Pompeii. Usually the slaves were brought to Pompeii from conquered countries. It was possible for a slave to buy, or be given, his freedom. If this happened, he and his descendants were known as *freedmen*. They had the full rights of citizens of the Roman Empire except for one thing—they could not hold public office. Many of the most successful businesses in Pompeii were owned by freedmen.

The lives of the poor were very different from their rich neighbors. Some people ran modest businesses in rented shops. Most of the shops were tiny. They had just two rooms. The front room facing the street was for the business. The shop owner and his family all lived crowded together in the dark, stuffy back room.

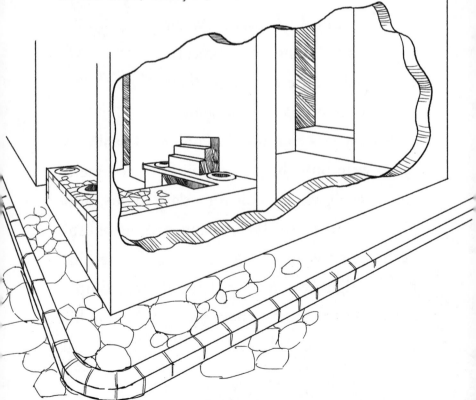

The poor had no kitchens, bathrooms, or toilets. Since the poor people had no way to cook their own food, they bought food at cookshops (which were like snack bars). There they could get stews, cheese, beans, or fish. The cooked food was kept warm in ceramic pots set into the shop's counter. Pompeians could eat their meals in the shop or take the cooked food home to eat with their families. All the garbage, including human waste, was thrown out into the street. Most of the streets did not have gutters, so the garbage just stayed there rotting and creating quite a stink.

The centers of the streets were raised so that a heavy rainfall could wash everything into a storm drain.

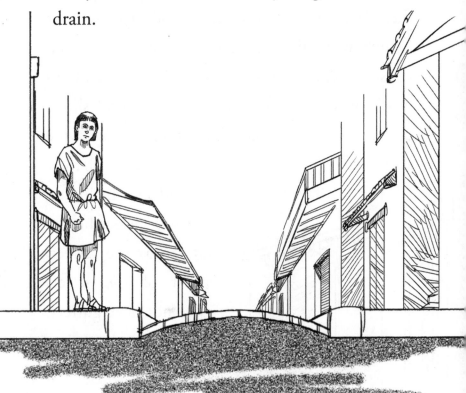

The streets in Pompeii also had raised stepping-stones so people could cross without stepping in garbage. Whenever wealthy Pompeiians went out, they wore shoes or boots to protect their feet from the filth and garbage in the streets and on the sidewalks. Their slave or servant would follow them carrying their sandals. They would change into their sandals once they reached their destinations.

## CHAPTER 8
## Public Places

The weather in Southern Italy is sunny and warm for most of the year, so the people of Pompeii spent a great deal of time outdoors. If they weren't at home or at work, townspeople would gather in public areas such as the Forum, the two theaters, the amphitheater, the many temples all over town, and the public baths.

The heart of Pompeii was the Forum, a group of buildings surrounding a large open rectangular area.

It measures approximately one hundred and fifty feet wide and five hundred feet long and is in the oldest part of Pompeii. Surrounded by at least forty statues of gods, military heroes, and emperors, the Forum had many purposes. Farmers brought their goods to the weekly market. On hot days teachers would bring their students and teach in the shade of the double-height colonnade that surrounded the Forum on three sides.

People also came to worship in the two main temples—the Temple of Apollo and the Temple of Jupiter, Juno, and Minerva. Another building, called the Basilica, housed law courts. This was where magistrates (judges) would hear cases and make rulings.

Magistrates were elected by the male citizens of Pompeii. Their job was to enforce laws passed by an assembly of one hundred men. These men were chosen from the most important families of Pompeii. The highest honor was to be elected patron. The patron represented Pompeii in Rome.

Politics was important to the citizens of Pompeii. Elections were held every year. At the time of the eruption, there were more than 2,500 election posters all over town, painted in red or black. Posters could be found on the walls of houses and shops along Pompeii's main streets.

Although women could not vote in elections or hold public office, they found ways to take part in political life, most often by campaigning for the election of their sons or family friends.

Some of the election posters bear messages from women. "Iunia asks for you to elect Helvius Sabinus" and "I beg you to elect Helvius Sabinus, worthy of public office. Maria asks this." The largest building in the Forum at Pompeii was called the Eumachia, after the woman who had it

built. There are two different inscriptions on the building identifying her as the donor. Eumachia also had a large statue of herself placed prominently inside the building. The building's exact purpose remains a mystery. Some archeologists believe that Eumachia was trying to help her son's political career by giving a magnificent building to the city.

## Cemeteries

One thing you won't see inside the city walls of Pompeii is a cemetery. This is because Roman law decreed that no person, no matter how rich or famous, could be buried inside a city. In Pompeii, tombs of the wealthy lined the roads leading to the

city. Some tombs were two stories tall. Just outside one of the gates is the tomb of Eumachia, the same Eumachia who sponsored the largest building in the Forum. The tomb she built for herself and her family is one of Pompeii's largest. It has two levels and a semicircular seating area where friends and relatives could rest when they came to pay their respects to the dead. Unfortunately, Eumachia died when Vesuvius erupted, so she never got to be buried inside her fancy tomb.

# CHAPTER 9
## Going to the Theater

The people of Pompeii enjoyed going to the theater, and they had two to choose from, located right next to each other.

The older, smaller theater was called the Odeon and was covered with a wooden roof. Twelve hundred people could sit in the semicircular rows of seats that faced an open stage. Besides plays, Pompeians could also attend concerts and lectures in the Odeon. The larger theater held 5,000 people. There was even room for an orchestra in front of the stage. On hot summer days, a large awning stretched over the entire theater to provide shade for spectators. Sometimes perfumed water would be sprayed on the audience. (This attraction was announced in advance to increase attendance.)

Theatergoers saw a variety of plays. Greek tragedies, Roman comedies, and pantomime were all popular. Pompeians loved to see slapstick farces, in which oafs, idiots, and stuck-up buffoons were ridiculed. If the play was a tragedy, actors wore masks with exaggerated frowns and sad expressions. When the play was a comedy, the face on the mask was usually smiling and happy.

Whether comedy or tragedy, all the actors

were men. Women were only allowed to perform in certain plays called *pantomimes*. Both theaters were located in the oldest part of Pompeii. This was where the earliest settlers built their houses. Unlike the rest of Pompeii, which is built on a grid system with streets running at right angles to each other, the streets in the oldest part run helter-skelter.

A plaster cast of a victim

A nineteenth-century photograph of Pompeii and Mount Vesuvius

A nineteenth-century photograph of a courtyard in a Pompeian house

Stepping stones across a street in Pompeii

A bronze gladiator's helmet from Pompeii

A mosaic of a guard dog at a villa's entrance, saying
*Cave Canem*, or "Beware of the Dog"

Archeological
workers with casts
of victims

Plaster casts
of Pompeian
victims

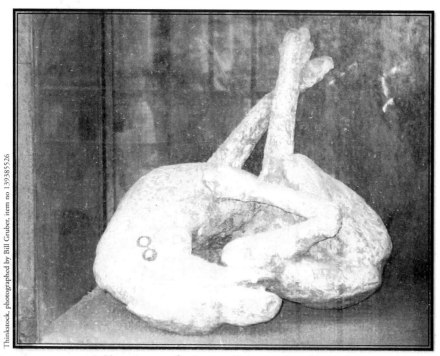

A plaster cast of a dog straining against his chain

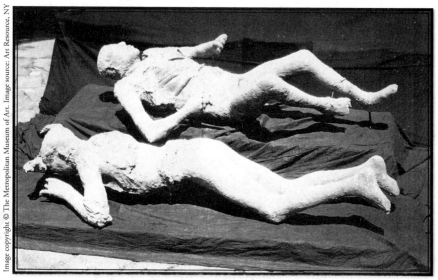

Plaster casts of victims

An eighteenth-century sketch of the view through
the Herculaneum Gate in Pompeii

A statue of Eumachia, one of Pompeii's
most prominent women

A mural in Pompeii,
showing the goddess of youth

A nineteenth-century
cameo pin made from lava

A portion of a mural in a Pompeian house

A household shrine of the god Jupiter

A mosaic from Pompeii

A Pompeian inn, with holes in the countertop to hold jars of wine or food

A cubiculum (or bedroom) with wall frescoes in a villa near Pompeii

A fountain in a Pompeian house

An amphitheater in Pompeii

A group of tourists at the Temple of Isis in the late nineteenth century

A modern-day photograph of Mount Vesuvius and the ruins of Pompeii

## CHAPTER 10
## Blood Sport

The oval amphitheater of Pompeii, seating 20,000 spectators, was one of the largest anywhere in the Roman Empire. The crowds who poured inside, climbing up outdoor stairways, did not come to see plays or listen to music. They came to watch professional fighters called *gladiators* battle against each other, often to the death.

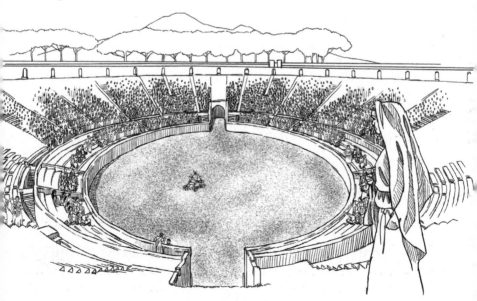

Gladiators were usually prisoners of war or condemned criminals. Some were poor men hoping to win wealth and glory. Most gladiators belonged to special schools where they were trained to fight. Gladiatorial games were extremely popular and often paid for by rich men who were running for office in Pompeii. They would put up painted signs announcing their sponsorship of the fights. One sign in Pompeii advertised, "Twenty pairs of gladiators of Quintus Monnius

Rufus will fight at Nola: 1, 2, 3 May. And there will be a hunt."

The best seats were those closest to the fighting. Spectators usually had to pay to sit there. Seats in the top eighteen rows of the amphitheater were free. Sometimes a generous sponsor would let everyone in for free.

The floor of the amphitheater was covered in sand to soak up blood from the fights. Often the opening acts pitted men armed only with daggers against wild animals such as tigers and bears. A tiger could easily tear a man apart; a bear could

kill a gladiator with merely a quick swipe of its paw. The main acts featured gladiator against gladiator. Some of the best fighters were as popular as movie stars are today. According to graffiti found on a wall in Pompeii, a gladiator named Celadus was "the man the girls sigh for." Try to imagine two men circling each other, weapons lifted, both ready to kill the other. Perhaps one is called Rufus, and the other is named Atticus. They are sweating and out of breath, because for the last fifteen minutes they have been engaged in a deadly battle.

In his left hand Rufus is holding a large fishing net made from rope. A shoulder guard protects his arm. In his right hand he carries a long, three-pronged lance called a *trident*. He is the type of gladiator called a *retiarius*. (You say it like this: reh-tee-air-ree-us.)His opponent, Atticus, is carrying a sharp two-edged sword and a long rectangular shield. A metal helmet protects his head. The helmet is smooth to make it harder for Rufus's net to snag it. Atticus is a type of gladiator known as a *secutor*. (You say it like this: seh-kyou-tore.)

Atticus, the secutor, is much more experienced than Rufus. He has fought fourteen fights and won them all. Rufus, the net man, has only fought two

matches. But so far he has been forcing Atticus to retreat. Then something unexpected happens. Atticus slips in the soft sand of the amphitheater. While he is down, Rufus quickly throws his net, which entraps Atticus, making it impossible for him to use his sword or shield. Rufus the retiarius

leaps forward and drives the sharpened points of his trident into his opponent's thigh.

The crowd is going wild! The secutor groans and drops his sword. He lies on his back while the retiarius stands above him, ready to deliver the final blow. Turning to the 20,000 spectators, Atticus holds up the index finger of his left hand. This gesture means that he is asking for mercy. The sponsor of that day's games is allowed to decide whether or not Rufus may go in for the kill. However, the custom is to let the spectators decide.

Luckily for Atticus, he is a favorite of this crowd. Pompeians have watched him fight and win many times before today. They also know that Rufus, the less experienced gladiator, got lucky. If Atticus hadn't slipped in the sand, it might well have been Rufus lying on the ground and gravely wounded. In a moment, thousands of hands are raised in the air. Practically everyone has their thumbs turned down. This is the signal that Atticus has hoped for. It means Rufus must put his weapon down and let Atticus live! No more blood will be shed between these two gladiators . . . at least not today.

# Types of Gladiators

In addition to secutors and retiarii, there were several other types of gladiators. Their names come from the type of armor they wore and the type of weapons they carried.

A *murmillo* wore a helmet with a fish motif, and carried a sword and shield.

A *hoplomachus* carried a lance and a short sword suitable for thrusting but not slashing. This kind of gladiator might also have a dagger, a

Murmillo      Hoplomachus      Samnite

small circular shield that really didn't offer much protection, and a helmet with a visor.

A Samnite carried a short sword and heavy shield, and wore an ornate helmet with a visor.

A *bestiarus* fought wild animals with spears and knives. For protection, a bestiarus might have nothing more than a small shield and helmet.

A Thracian carried a short curved sword and small shield. All Thracians wore helmets with a wide brim and a visor. The helmet usually was decorated with a crest of a griffin, a mythical creature with the body, tail, and back legs of a lion and the head and wings of an eagle.

Bestiarus          Thracian

# CHAPTER 11
## Cleaning Up

Since hardly any houses, even those of the very rich, had bathrooms, nearly all Pompeians went to one of the three public bathhouses to get themselves clean. The baths were large and

lavish and only charged a small fee. (The biggest was at the crossing of Pompeii's two main streets; another was very close to the Forum.)

At each of the public baths, men and women had their own separate areas with changing rooms, toilets, outdoor exercise space, and rooms with hot, warm, or cold water. Visitors left their clothes and belongings in a changing room. Men might first choose to go to a gymnasium to exercise. After working up a good sweat they would return to the changing room. Attendants would scrape off dirt and sweat with a tool called a *strigil* and then give their customers a massage.

Later it might be time to take a swim in the pool or spend time in the baths, which were each kept at a different temperature. There was a hot steamy room, the *caldarium*; a warm room called the *tepidarium*; and a small circular room, the *frigidarium*, where men took a plunge into cold water. The women's part of the bath only had a

caldarium and tepidarium. A small cold bath was part of their changing room, while the men had a separate, lavish frigidarium instead.

The baths had furnace rooms that heated the water. Hot air from the furnaces was channeled underneath the stone floors of the warm and hot rooms. The floor was so hot that bathers had to wear wooden-soled sandals to protect their feet from burning. Besides keeping Pompeians clean and healthy, the public bath was a place where people could socialize. They could gossip, argue about politics, or discuss the most recent matches between gladiators.

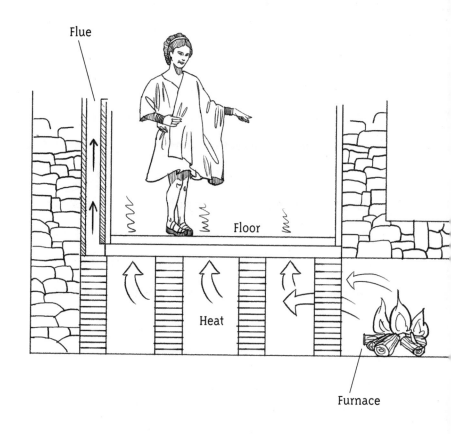

Flue

Floor

Heat

Furnace

# The Aqueduct

Pompeii had a plentiful supply of freshwater, thanks to a twenty-five-mile-long *aqueduct*. (An aqueduct is a system for carrying a large amount of water.) The aqueduct replaced Pompeians' dependence on getting water from the Sarno River or from wells. Water from the aqueduct came to the city through lead pipes and into a building where it was funneled in three directions.

Some water went to Pompeii's many public fountains, some went to the public baths, and some went directly into the homes of the wealthy. There were so many public fountains in Pompeii that archeologists say no citizen had to walk farther than ninety yards to get freshwater.

# CHAPTER 12
# Herculaneum

Pompeii was not the only city destroyed by the eruption of Vesuvius in 79 AD. Herculaneum was a small resort town where wealthy Romans built villas overlooking the Bay of Naples. Like Pompeii, Herculaneum disappeared and quickly was forgotten. But unlike Pompeii, Herculaneum was not covered up by ash and pumice. Instead, it was encased in something called *pyroclastic flow*, a fast-moving (up to 450 miles an hour!) mixture of hot gas and rock. It descended like an avalanche and in an instant burned the people of Herculaneum to a crisp. Only their bones remained.

When the pyroclastic flow cooled, it hardened like solid concrete. This made excavation much

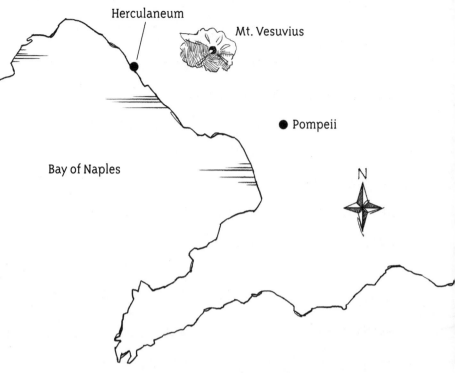

Herculaneum

Mt. Vesuvius

● Pompeii

Bay of Naples

N

more difficult than at Pompeii. The first evidence of the buried city turned up in 1710 when a farmer digging a well near a town called Resina uncovered slabs of marble. After that, a rich local landowner hired men to dig tunnels into the site to find marble to decorate his new home. When the home was finished, he had the tunnels blocked and work stopped. Then, in 1738, marble slabs with the inscription *Theatrum Herculanensi* (the Theater of Herculaneum) were found. Now the buried city had a name.

Because excavating at Herculaneum has always proved so difficult, most of the city has been left just as it was. Even today, 75 percent of Herculaneum remains buried. Still, there have been some important discoveries.

A very large villa was uncovered, and it is one of the largest Roman villas ever found. Over 250 yards long, the villa has beautiful gardens, many fountains, and over eighty magnificent sculptures. The villa also contained a library of nearly 1,800 ancient scrolls. But the heat of the pyroclastic

Villa at Herculaneum

flow turned the scrolls into carbon. While more than two million tourists visit Pompeii every year, only about 320,000 make a stop at Herculaneum. One reason is that because of the difficulty of excavation, there is not nearly as much to see. But another reason is that a modern city, Ercolano, sits right on top of much of the ruins.

# CHAPTER 13
## Pompeii Today

Although Pompeii is a tremendously popular tourist site, for many visitors it is a disappointing experience. Large sections of Pompeii are closed to visitors because they are unsafe.

Today the city of Pompeii is in grave danger. Buildings have been collapsing. In November 2010, the walls of the gladiator barracks crumbled overnight into piles of bricks. This and other collapses are the result of years of neglect and mismanagement. Poor maintenance of Pompeii's buildings have left valuable artifacts exposed to the elements. Without adequate protection, mosaics and frescoes disintegrate, roofs cave in, and walls crumble. Herculaneum had been experiencing the same problems. Two-thirds of the ruins were closed to visitors. Wall collapses and flaking frescoes were common.

Today, thanks to the combined efforts of British, American, and Italian art organizations, Herculaneum is in great shape. New areas of the ruins are being opened to tourists, and archeologists and art conservators have taken a new approach to solving Herculaneum's problems.

Because water and humid conditions were the

cause of most of the damage to the buildings and artwork, protective roofing was installed wherever it was needed. Ancient storm drains and sewers were opened up to direct groundwater away from the buildings.

Once that was accomplished, conservators were able to restore important frescoes and mosaics, and buildings that were about to collapse have been stabilized and reopened to the public.

Now the Italian Government, with funding from UNESCO (The United Nations Educational, Scientific, and Cultural Organization) says it will follow the Herculaneum model at Pompeii. Incompetent managers have been fired, drainage will be improved, and additional restorers will be hired and trained to work at Pompeii. This is welcome news for anyone interested in Roman art, architecture, and history. There is simply no place like Pompeii anywhere else on our planet.

# Timeline of Pompeii

| | |
|---|---|
| ~800 BC | The Greeks settle near Pompeii |
| 80 BC | Pompeii is established as a Roman colony |
| 59 AD | Riots occur at the amphitheatre |
| 62 AD | An earthquake originating below Vesuvius severely damages Pompeii |
| 79 AD | Vesuvius erupts, burying Pompeii, Herculaneum, and surrounding areas |
| 1748 | The first formal excavations of Pompeii begin |
| 1763 | Discovery of a plaque that officially identifies the ruins as the ancient city of Pompeii |
| 1848 | Giuseppe Fiorelli completes his initial excavations in Pompeii |
| 1860 | Giuseppe Fiorelli becomes director of excavations in Pompeii |
| 1943 | Pompeii is bombed by the Allies during World War II |
| 1944 | Vesuvius erupts |
| 1980 | An earthquake near Vesuvius causes damage to the ruins of Pompeii |
| 1997 | A special law is passed that says all money taken at the gates in Pompeii must go toward conserving the ruins |
| 2011 | A major initiative to conserve the houses of Pompeii begins |

# Timeline of the World

| | |
|---|---|
| Rome becomes a republic | 509 BC |
| Spartacus leads a slave rebellion against Rome | 73 BC |
| Julius Caesar is named dictator for life, then is assassinated on the Ides of March | 44 BC |
| The construction of the Roman Colosseum is completed | 80 AD |
| The First Crusade begins | 1096 |
| Christopher Columbus sails to the New World in first of four voyages | 1492 |
| Michelangelo finishes the famous fresco that covers the Sistine Chapel's ceiling | 1512 |
| The *Mayflower* lands in Plymouth Rock | 1620 |
| On July 4, thirteen American colonies declare independence from England | 1776 |
| Krakatoa erupts in Indonesia | 1883 |
| The largest eruption of the twentieth century occurs at Novarupta in Alaska | 1912 |
| Italy joins the Allies in World War I | 1915 |
| Daily newspaper comic strip *Superman* debuts | 1939 |
| The Axis Powers (Germany, Italy, and Japan) are defeated, bringing World War II to an end | 1945 |
| Mount Saint Helens erupts in Washington | 1980 |
| Eyjafjallajökull erupts in Iceland | 2010 |

# Bibliography

Amery, Colin, and Brian Curran Jr. *The Lost World of Pompeii.*
Los Angeles: J. Paul Getty Museum, 2002.

Beard, Mary. *The Fires of Vesuvius: Pompeii Lost and Found.*
Cambridge, MA: Belknap Press of Harvard University Press,
2008.

Berry, Joanne. *The Complete Pompeii.* New York: Thames &
Hudson, 2007.

Brown, Dale, ed. *Pompeii: The Vanished City.* Alexandria, VA:
Time-Life Books, 1992.

Cooley, Alison E., and M. G. L. Cooley. *Pompeii: A Sourcebook.*
London: Routledge, 2004.

Zanker, Paul. *Pompeii: Public and Private Life.* Translated by
Deborah Lucas Schneider. Cambridge, MA: Harvard University
Press, 1998.

## Videos

"Herculaneum Uncovered." *Secrets of the Dead.* Season 6, episode 3. DVD. Directed by Richard Bedser. Aired May 2, 2004. Alexandria, VA: PBS Home Video, 2007.

Kleiner, Diane E. E. **"Lifestyles of the Rich and Famous: Houses and Villas at Pompeii."** Filmed Spring 2009. Open Yale Courses video, 75:30. Posted September 14, 2009. http://oyc.yale.edu/history-art/hsar-252/lecture-5.

*Lost Treasures of the Ancient World: Pompeii: The Doomed City.* Directed by Bob Carruthers. West Long Branch, NJ: Kultur Video, 2006.